D0001865

Logophilia

poems by

Mimi Herman

MAIN STREET RAG PUBLISHING COMPANY
CHARLOTTE, NORTH CAROLINA

The author gratefully acknowledges the following publications
where these poems first appeared, sometimes in different versions:

> *The Best of the Fuquay-Varina Reading Series:* "Gretel,"
> "It's Not That I Don't Like You,"
> "On the Importance of Explanatory Text"
> *Hawai'i Review:* "Things Undone Around the House,"
> "The Storm"
> *The Hollins Critic:* "The Foreman at the Self-Doubt Factory"
> *Main Street Rag:* "Last Bout"
> *North Carolina Arts Council Website:* "Fill Her Up,"
> "On the Importance of Explanatory Text"
> *Wild Goose Poetry Review:* "Cassandra," "The Visualizing Mind
> Has No Word for No," "Warner Brothers Physics"

ISBN: 978-1-59948-388-7

Produced in the United States of America

Main Street Rag Publishing Company
PO BOX 690100
Charlotte, NC 28227-7001
www.MainStreetRag.com

For John, my family and all my reader and writer friends.
With thanks to Malaika.

Contents

The Visualizing Mind Has No Word for No

Try not to think of a banana.

Whatever you do, do not imagine a banana
with its greeny-yellow peel
and firm flesh.

Or one that has succumbed
to brown spots and a certain laxness of texture.

Please, under no circumstances,
imagine a banana, a single banana
on your kitchen counter.

Where there is also, coincidentally, not
a piece of chocolate cake, thick with frosting,
the last piece of chocolate cake, as alluring
as a showgirl leaning against the backstage door
asking if you can give her a lift.

Say to yourself, I will not eat that piece of chocolate cake,
that last piece. I don't need it.
And as soon as you've opened your mouth, it's gone,
startling you with the swiftness
with which each bite leaps onto the fork and is conveyed
to your mouth, to descend down some long dark road
that leads directly to your hips,
where it will take up residence for a good long time

because morning after morning you will remind
yourself not to sleep in, and will miss the gym,
which is probably not a bad idea
since it gives you more time to tell your children
not to touch the stove and to get out the salve
that you'll surely need.

Fill Her Up

You fill me up like a Pop-Tart fills the toaster,
sweet and hot.
You're every recipe my grandmother made
and I forgot.
You're all my lost relatives
come home again.
You're my old address, my old dress—the one I wore
to the ninth grade prom.
You're my virginity come back to haunt me.
You're new rains, old pains, cinquains I wrote
in the fourth grade. You're every note
I ever passed.

You are a branch bank opening in my neighborhood
with free lifetime incomes to the first one hundred customers.
You're a high like exercise (if exercise behaved as advertised),
like hitting butter halfway down the popcorn bucket,
like staying in the movie for a double feature
I didn't even pay for.

You're a microscope that sees through my skin,
a telescope that lets me keep my distance.

You fill me up like premium gas at Costco
caught before the cost goes up.
All that power in my tank—and at such a savings.
You fill me up like the first snow
fills the junkyards clean again.
A million flakes to cover one defunct Caddy
and suddenly it's young again.
It runs again.

Logophilia

I love everything about words,
the way they roll across the palate
and off the tongue,
the way the sometimes unpalatable ones
can't be swallowed, like Demosthenes' stones.
They sweeten the bitter, they sour the sweet.

I love the way words mate in my mouth,
butter and fingers, even and song,
or play in the park,
the way jump and rope join
and go skipping down the street.

I even like the way words can wound the sound,
as when I wound my watch, when tick turned into tock.
The click of a clock is enough to send me spinning.

There are days when I hover above
my love for words, even
the words I've befriended,
before I'm brave and dive,
before I've descended
into the way words can easily mean
other than what they intended.

Microscope

With two hands, as she has been taught,
the girl lifts the microscope from its black leather box,
hoists it to the kitchen table, pulls up the stool for height
and kneels, left hand holding her left eye shut,
peering through the lens with her right.

She may turn the knob a fraction
and overshoot clarity.
When she gets the adjustment just wrong
her own lashes sweep back in her vision
like a giant slow-moving sea creature.

She makes slides of slices: leaves, green or dead,
thin slivers of apple, scraps of onionskin,
the occasional drop—with held breath
and one of her mother's embroidery needles—of blood.

The cells swim in her blood like indolent bathers,
slower and slower until they die,
drowned by light.

She sometimes imagines that the god her parents pray to
is a girl like her, kneeling on a stool,
eye pressed to the lens of a bigger microscope.
That girl, stool and all, and parents and world
swimming in the immense gap between slide and cover slip.

The cells beneath her microscope
also gods.

Role Models

I look to the stout women in exercise class,
hips stuffed into leggings
like whipped cream in a pastry tube.
They move as if to say
I have all my own operating instructions.

You never hear them apologize
for their waistlines spilling
over the elastic bands of their exercise pants,
their breasts crammed like a couple of afterthoughts
into overstretched black exercise bras.

You never see them apologize
by refusing to look in the mirror.
When you catch their eyes, they smile.
The mirror loves them.
The teacher loves them.
The music wants to run its fingers
over their purple Lycra leggings
and linger.

While my body,
enemy of the state
of mind to which I wish
to emigrate,
bows and scrapes
its half-assed punches and kicks.

But my vicious internal trainer can't resist
dwelling on the slender,
the twenty-one-year-old willows
who weave and bend
while I crack and wend
my way as far from the mirror
as I can be and still remain
in class.

How can I not love the zaftig and stout,
the what it's all about ladies
who are twice my size and attitude
and move as if to say
Who can resist
My kick and luscious sway?

It's Not That I Don't Like You

It's not that I don't like you.
It's just that I prefer to address you
through this bulletproof glass, which
if you don't mind
I'll ask you to keep clean on your side.

Here is the Windex, and here the sterile cloth
I've had delivered to you in a box
I did not pack with my own two hands.
Careful there.
You missed a spot.

Yes, I'd be delighted
to spend the evening with you,
as soon as I slip into
something a bit more
invulnerable.

There Goes the Neighborhood

What is your liver doing
when you're not looking?
And those lungs of yours?
You try to keep them well aired,
but even when you forget,
someone keeps running the city.

Millions of parasites cling to your skin,
take up residence in the tenements
of your internal organs
without paying rent.
They leave their effluence
and move on to another neighborhood
in a nicer part of the city
or die, unmourned,
on the stomach floor.

Who's the mayor?
Even when you're busy,
even when you're lying in bed,
even when, as now,
you put down this book
and close your eyes,
someone is paying off the sanitation engineers
while someone else is flushing the sewers.

To whom have you subcontracted
your right elbow joint?
The running of your knees?
Who is the crossing guard of your larynx,
the cop keeping traffic moving
through your large intestine?

A billion billion cells
seem to know what they're doing.
They punch their time cards and go to work
knowing another billion billion scabs
are waiting to take their jobs
for lower pay.

Except sometimes
when a whole neighborhood goes dark
leaving you with a heart that murmurs
sweet nothing, sweet nothing, sweet nothing.

God is Not a Short-Order Cook

God is not a short-order cook.
You can't ask for one marriage, over easy,
or your enemy, scrambled.
Can't wave the waitress to your booth
and demand the healthy kid special, extra syrup.

In the same way, God won't whip up
an end to war while you wait,
won't turn down the heat on global warming
or slip the wrong political party out of the frying pan
and into the fire.

We line up at the counter, yelling our orders,
our asses pinched by the rips in the vinyl stools,
trying to be heard over the jukebox,
which is twanging out country and western
heartbreak, two for a quarter.

Meanwhile, God has hung up the egg-stained apron
walked out back where it's cooler
and quiet enough to hear all the voices in this diner
or any other and everywhere else
Dopplering like distant traffic

on a road where God is not the driver
but the road itself, and the dirt underneath,
the air molecules crowding and distancing in turn
and all the grass that used to live where the road now runs
and will grow after we are gone.

How to Say No

Practice it plain,
unadorned
and completely
unmourned.
Not *No, thank you*
or *I'm sorry, but no,*
but no
as it is, no sugar
to sweeten it,
no cream
to soften it.
Take it hot and
take it black,
but whatever you do,
don't
take it back.

The Fairy Tale Emotion Series

Loneliness
Jack without Jill,
with pail, without water.
Hill? Yes, but
no tumbling after.

Hope
One damned shoe,
two damned sisters,
an old lady who
dumps you in a pumpkin.
You wait for him to want you
enough to try to find you.
Hope is a thing that blisters.

Fear
The wolf's teeth glisten with spit.
This is not your grandmother,
just the skin she was in
and the small square of light
where she once lived.

Desire
Just two ruby
lips, two apple
cheeks, one alabaster glove
of skin all over my body.

Just a curtain of ebony
hair, two emerald
eyes, this beauty
that she's hardly using.

That's all I ask.

Miriam

He wasn't a bad kid for a baby,
but he cried a lot and, being the boy,
got all the attention.
I wasn't sorry to send him reeling down the river
in the bulrush basket
I wove as a project in art class.

History says I was brave and good,
but history is a braggart.
Really, I was just as glad to see the last of him.

Let something go
and pretty soon you want it back.
I hid among the rushes,
watched those girls bathe and giggle.

When the basket floated by, she thought it was a gift
from a secret admirer, just the sort of thing
she'd expect from the nerdy boy who sat behind her in geometry,

calculating the angle of the hypotenuse, wind speed,
the rate of the Nile's drift,
to aim that baby straight at the girl with the kohl-rimmed eyes.

My brother was never more than a doll to her
and my mother, wet-nurse to a damp baby,
just an accessory
in the dollhouse that was Egypt.

Cassandra

Cassandra was very popular at parties
for the first five minutes.
After that, guests tired of her tricks.
The teenagers peeled off for spin the bottle,
the grown-ups for poker.

Everyone prefers a game of chance
where you win or lose big.
Who wants to know the outcome in advance?

Which is why we forgot what she said
and what her voice sounded like, or even,
eventually, the color of her hair
and whether she was long-waisted with thin lips
or thick-waisted with a long nose.

Which is why, no matter how often she told us what would happen,
we bet over and over on the same bad hand
as if it were a foreign verb we forced ourselves to conjugate,
never getting the tenses right.

Which is why, after awhile,
no one invited her to parties
and we, playing long odds with a short deck,
lost to the house of history every time.

Eleanor

Not known for introspection,
I got things done.
My mother turned her face away
when I nursed.
Frank didn't marry me for my looks,
which was fine.
I didn't marry him for his, either.

They said the women
should have bothered me,
but Frank kept them well in hand
and some things, well, let's say
I understood.
You make up for a loss where you can.

Not beautiful, of course,
but I was the figurehead of the ship of state.
As we plowed through seas of war and poverty,
I was the virtue we sought to inculcate.

Gretel

I parceled out the crumbs for pigeons
not—as you thought, Hansel—to find the way home.
Home was a shuttered cupboard.
I was a gumdrop girl
grateful to find that sugar lick.

The witch didn't understand.
I'd have done anything
to be like her: devil on one shoulder, devil on the other,
hair tied back, knotted in a piece of butcher's string
still bloody from the meat she slapped on the table
for our supper.

I ate it raw.

Digging into it with my child-fingers,
my nails neatly trimmed
as if I'd had a mother
or a father who cared.
I could not wait for her to sear the steak.

After supper I dipped my hands in the well,
dyeing the water pink.
The witch sniffed at my palm,
her mouth a pursed slash of licorice.
When she tasted, tentative, a finger,
her lollipop eyes went wide.
She rushed from the room.

Hansel, you edge around the ginger walls,
hedging when I ask
Why are you afraid?
I'm just tired, you say.

But you sleep with your eyes open
like the dead we've lost from living too much.
I press your eyes shut,
but still you watch me
as I look backward with a hunger
breadcrumbs will not satisfy.

The Foreman at the Self-Doubt Factory

There's never enough self-doubt in the world
so I manufacture more,
cranking it out in my basement factory
night and day, available globally.

An assembly line takes care of obsessions,
welding the things you should have said
to the ways people can't stand you:
too difficult, too distant, too needy, too whiny.

Another line stacks your failures,
one atop the last,
then threads in a rusty rod of rejection
neatly screwing you over.

Then there are your looks.
I've had to add an entire annex for those,
to make mirrors to amplify your hips and zits
and pants than shrink sadistically in your closet while you sleep.

In shorthand, my secretaries note down each stupid comment you
                    ever made
and will, upon request, repeat it back to you with unerring precision.
They even get the intonation right,
adding just a modicum of self-mockery.

There is nothing I wouldn't do
in the interest of humanity
though I sometimes question whether I'm qualified
to demean us sufficiently.

Last Bout

Anxiety pinions me
like an out-of-shape wrestler.
Forget how much I can bench.
I'm not even in his weight class.

Sweating, he pins me to the ropes,
his bleached blond mullet slick with grease.
His ham hock forearms press the breath from my chest.
He's got me where he wants me, slumped

against the ropes creasing my back muscles,
heart pumping against his slick shaved pecs.
He doesn't want me to make a comeback.
He loves to see his name over mine on the marquee.

He wears the yellow satin.
He wears the 14 carat gold trophy on a red, white and blue ribbon.
He wears me down to the frayed tendon
of the Achilles heel of my pride.

I drag myself to my basement dressing room
where the mirror spits back my reflection,
while out in the stands, the fans stampede,
a million disillusioned feet stomping the torn tickets

that bore my name.

Stitches

A stitch in time
saves nine,
but what of the nine
neglected stitches
standing in the wings?
They, too,
want to sing.

They've learned their lines,
their entrances,
while waiting for
that solitary stitch
just once to miss its cue.

In deference
to lesser things,
it might be worth
considering
the freshness
understudies bring
to the same old lines.

and perhaps
the soloist,
that prima donna
of a stitch,
might learn, in turn,
humility
in being saved by nine.

Bedtime Story

Every night I tuck in bed
the daughter that I haven't had,
then sit up talking by the fire
with the son that I desire.

We talk until the fire stills
its angry cracks and war of wills.
We talk about his college plans.
The coals make shoals of our dark hands.

Upstairs, my daughter's sleepy murmurs
unlatch the catch, and moonlight glimmers
softly in my open throat—
a window opened up to hope.

While outside in the dark you stand,
a gift for me within each hand,
looking in and wondering whether
we can live this life together.

Teachable Moments

We can't resist them, like Easter eggs
strewn through the back yard
of our lives with children.

We like to remove them from the grass
where they lie, half-hidden,
and cry, *See! Here's one!*

Then we unpeel their brightly-dyed shells
to reveal to the children
The perfectly hard-boiled nutrition inside.

No matter how good for them, it's never
the solid chocolate they really wanted
or the chick that, had we waited, might have pecked its way out.

On the Importance of Explanatory Text

I am the sort of person who stands
on the edge of the Grand Canyon
and reads the educational plaque
before looking down.

Even in museums, I experience vertigo
if I stare straight at a painting
without first grounding myself in the title, artist, dates of birth
     and death
and the various media involved in producing the piece.
A little interpretive verbiage is never lost on me.

I need words first to appreciate the mystery
of art or beauty, which is why
I have requested that you take a few minutes from your day
to compose a series of labels I can use
to keep from being overwhelmed with dizziness
at the sight of you in repose
or standing by the stove stirring eggs
or lifting one hundred fifty pounds over your head
or suddenly in a crowd
where I hadn't expected you to be.

I need a label on the dashboard of your car
and another on the headboard of my bed
and to be prepared
should I survive you
which, if you don't mind, I'd prefer not to do,
could you make just one more label
to place above your headstone?
Something simple and complete
that will help me understand,
that will keep the vertigo at bay
so I won't fall off the earth
you're buried in.

The Storm

The storm raged without thunder
like a debarked dog
chasing out the usual
Bay Area fog.

Pelleted with stinging rain,
every roof rang back,
vicious precipitation
and counterattack.

The winds battered the windows.
Glass rattled in frames.
Water welled up in the streets.
We forgot our names.

Warner Brothers Physics

It is the fear of death that quickens us
to call and say, *I was just thinking of you.*
but it isn't you we were thinking of exactly.
It is the moment when the *not-you, ever again*
will open its gigantic hole beneath us
that we've suddenly recognized.

But, as if gravity were dependent on
the acknowledgement of gravity,
as if cartoons gave us
a truer portrait of our psyches than Freud,
a truer physics than Isaac Newton,
Wile E. Coyote about to Doppler toward the center of the earth,
Uh-oh,
we hang suspended.

We see that hole. We don't want to fall.
So when you are surprised to hear me call,
out of breath, to say, *I thought of you*
know that I am reinventing the physics of your existence.
Know that I mean, *I want you to live.*

Apnea

You breathe beside me quietly,
then suddenly don't breathe at all.
I wake in panic. Shallow heaves
are followed by a click. In awe
I listen to the fruitless breaths
that will not travel to your lungs,
unconsummated little deaths.
On each inhale my own breath hangs.
When finally the air completes
its journey, the alveoli
can do their job and then release
the CO_2. You shudder. Why
should breathing be a nightly risk,
each breath a death you barely miss?

Yeast

In the refrigerator sits the yeast,
bottle darkened to forestall quickening.
It wants to be born. The nature of the beast
is to bubble into life, then, thickening,
to reproduce and reproduce again.
Like an embryo, it grows by doubling.
The bread bowl curves, a womb the dough grows in
to keep it safe. The world is troubling,
but yeast when it grows up wants to be bread.
Its adolescence is the awkward dough,
which flinches when it's punched, and ducks its head,
inclined to burrow back into the bowl,
and when it's aged, it grows a harder crust.
Yeast quickens, thickens, hardens. Then it's dust.

The Death of a Best Friend

You can't claim credit for it
the way you could if—God forbid—
you lost your wife or child.

At the funeral, if this is a good week for your arthritis,
you will be one of six pallbearers
to carry his remnants
where you don't want him to go.
Or if your joints won't let you,
you'll sit in the row behind his wife and children.

He was the only one who saw you whole.
Each of you thought the other
was the better artist.
The fact that you could talk shop together
kept the shop open.
You loved him—if love isn't too strong a word
and now it isn't, though
you wish you could have said it then
when he could have heard.

In a closet of your heart
deep, disorganized, though not dark,
are strewn all the conversations you were going to have,
now slipped off their hangers, wrinkled.

Your wife loves you, but she'd willingly help you
clean out this closet if you'd let her.

You used to wear this friendship like an old coat
that finally fit when the seams got frayed.
Holes in the pockets from the secrets you carried for him
like smooth river stones.
He had a coat just the same.

And if it comforts you, I'll tell you,
he's wearing it now.

Do Not Disturb

The wren at the birdfeeder by opening the door,
the willow oak leaves tangled in a web
outside your living room window
even though they make you feel like the bad housekeeper
you suspect you are,

two or more people in an argument,
a dam a six-year-old has made of sticks
in the creek at the bottom of your street,
a cake in flight in the oven, rising,
sleeping cats—or mating horses—
a wall of drying paint, a dying insect,
a man, crying.

Funeral in the Rain

In the limousine, the mourners are arguing
about who will pick up the kids after this.
Just ahead, a policeman holds opposing lines
of traffic at bay with both hands. People in cars
who haven't felt the loss of anything but time
are required to wait to let this procession pass.

Black cars, like hard-carapaced beetles,
give way to floating rows of black umbrellas.
In high-heeled pumps and polished black lace-ups
the mourners pick their way across the wet grass,
avoiding patches of mud or slippery gravel.
When they look up, the grave comes as a surprise.

A heavy silvered mahogany box poised
on woven yellow belts above the hole.
Concealed by a blue tarp, a pile of dirt.
A tent just big enough to hold
those most closely linked by DNA or law.
Those farther and less dear adjust their umbrellas
to repel the rain's new slant.

Mumbles of eulogy, murmurs of grief
punctuated by hard punches of *loss* and *leaves behind*.
Then the litany of names, begats abandoned by their begetter.
The mourners stand by the grave in clutches,
some grave themselves, some biding time until the ceremony ends.
Everyone forgets how grief works. It's not until
the earth drops from your fingers and thuds on the coffin

or some months later when you pick up the phone to call
a number that is *no longer in service at this time*
or, quite often, as you're washing dishes,
your hands clammy in yellow gloves,
the water running unheeded over greasy pans and glasses,
that you'll drop into the hole the grave made into the rain
where your heart will begin to decompose in the box of your chest.

Things Undone Around the House

The bushes need trimming.
They've needed trimming for six months.
Dust bunnies hang out beneath my sofa
where they play endless poker games
for the change they find under the cushions.

The porch hasn't been swept
since the willow oak pollinated.
No, let's be honest —
since last fall when the oak lost its leaves.

The bathtub is as yellow as a bad tooth
and I can't remember the last time
I brushed my hair
or looked in the mirror
with anything resembling kindness.

The Dead Bury the Dead

The dead are burying the dead
with small abandoned shovels borrowed
from children's sandcastles.

Remarkably patient, they dig until dawn,
then replace the shovels in time
for the mothers, over breakfast, to remind

the children to bring in their toys.
Boys will, in fact, be boys
and girls will remain girls,

while the dead remake the world as we sleep,
knowing it is their job to keep
grief buried, one small shovelful at a time.

All the Lost Words

I don't like to believe
that I am getting older
and losing words
because that's what we older people do.

Or, heaven forbid,
that I have been invaded
by a small, non-malignant but stubborn tumor
that has ensconced itself at the precise ganglion
that leads to the tip of my tongue.

It is indeed possible
that I have always been forgetful,
but that I've somehow forgotten
just how forgetful I was.

But I prefer to believe
that I have unwittingly located a snag
in the fabric of the universe
like the one located beneath the ribs of your dryer
through which socks slip—singly, sadly—

only to emerge into the gentle light of a companion universe
where people walk around warm in mismatched socks
uttering all those wise words
I meant to have said.

Pause

To take a vacation from time, I began by unpacking
the appointment calendar from my briefcase,
my grandfather's wristwatch from my jewelry bag.

I went on to cancel my airline reservations,
pulled the plug on all the traffic lights in town
and shattered my speedometer.

Before the first day was over, I'd discarded
every box of instant oatmeal from the pantry,
disconnected my timing belt and sent the sun south for the winter.

That night, I unpinned the moon from the sky's collar,
shook the wrinkles from the tides
until the sea was as crisp as the starched linen sheets

on which I slept, after I detached my heart
and stilled the tongue of the metronome,
so it would stop repeating your name.